SPORTS' WILDEST UPSETS

PRO BASEBALL UPSETS

JEFF SEIDEL

Lerner Publications ◆ Minneapolis

Lerner Publications Company
An imprint of Lerner Publishing Group, Inc.
241 First Avenue North
Minneapolis, MN 55401 USA

For reading levels and more information, look up this title at www.lernerbooks.com.

Main body text set in Aptifer Sans LT Pro.
Typeface provided by Linotype AG.

Library of Congress Cataloging-in-Publication Data
ISBN 978-1-5415-7710-7 (lib. bdg.)
ISBN 978-1-5415-8965-0 (pbk.)
ISBN 978-1-5415-8367-2 (eb pdf)

Manufactured in the United States of America
1 – CG – 12/31/19

CONTENTS

Whether it's a team's first title or their 27th, winning the World Series is always exciting.

FIRST PITCH

GREAT UPSETS ARE ONE REASON BASEBALL IS ONE OF THE MOST POPULAR SPORTS IN THE UNITED STATES. Each baseball team plays 162 regular-season games, the most in any professional sport. This means there are many chances for low-ranked teams to beat league powerhouses.

The World Series is a best-of-seven series between the American League (AL) and National League (NL) champions at the end of the baseball season. The first team to win four games is the champion. The World Series is often filled with drama. Any team has the chance to be the best.

Players, coaches, and managers all say the game is not finished until the last out is made. There are many times when teams have **rallied** late in a game or a series to surprise the other team and everyone watching.

FACTS AT A GLANCE

- The Boston Red Sox trailed the New York Yankees three games to none in the 2004 American League Championship Series (ALCS), but they came back to win. It was the first—and as of 2018 the only—time in Major League Baseball (MLB) history that a team won a series after being down three games to none.

- Before 1969, the New York Mets never had a winning record. But that year, the Mets reached the World Series and won against the Baltimore Orioles.

- Bill Mazeroski hit a home run to end Game 7 of the 1960 World Series. This gave the Pittsburgh Pirates the championship over the New York Yankees, the most dominant team in baseball at the time.

GIANTS' MARATHON WIN

THE 2014 WASHINGTON NATIONALS HAD THE BEST RECORD IN THE NL. With stars Bryce Harper and Stephen Strasburg, Washington was the heavy **favorite** against the San Francisco Giants in the best-of-five NL Division Series.

Bryce Harper was the Washington Nationals' top hitter during the 2014 postseason.

But the Giants beat the odds and won Game 1. In Game 2, San Francisco made history. The Nationals led 1–0 at the top of the ninth inning. Washington's Jordan Zimmerman was on fire. He had thrown eight scoreless innings. But then San Francisco's Buster Posey got on base and teammate Pablo Sandoval hit a double to tie the score.

Eight more innings passed without either team scoring. That's when the Giants finally broke through. First baseman Brandon Belt hit a homer. The Giants kept their lead and won. Lasting 18 innings, it was the longest MLB postseason game ever.

FINAL SERIES SCORE

GIANTS	NATIONALS
3	1

Many expected the New York Yankees to win the 1960 World Series, but the Pittsburgh Pirates fought them hard until the final pitch.

PIRATES BEAT BASEBALL'S BEST

THE NEW YORK YANKEES WERE THE FAVORITE GOING INTO THE 1960 WORLD SERIES. Baseball's best team had won seven of the previous 11 World Series. But the Pittsburgh Pirates weren't scared. They knew they had the team that could beat the Yankees.

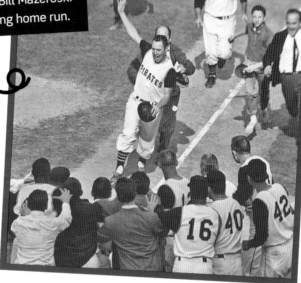

Each team won three of the first six games. The championship came down to the final inning of Game 7. The score was tied 9–9. Bill Mazeroski was the Pirates' first batter in the bottom of the ninth. He wasn't known for his hitting. But that was all about to change.

Mazeroski swung at the second pitch from the Yankees' Ralph Terry. Crack! The ball soared into the air and over the left-field fence. Fans poured onto the field as Mazeroski raced around the bases. The Pirates had just won the game 10–9. They also won the World Series, beating the mighty Yankees.

FINAL SERIES SCORE

PIRATES | YANKEES

4 | 3

ORIOLES PITCH THE DODGERS

FEW TEAMS COULD MATCH THE LOS ANGELES DODGERS IN 1966. Ace pitchers Sandy Koufax and Don Drysdale had led the team to 95 wins. Most expected the Dodgers to beat the Baltimore Orioles and claim a second World Series title in a row.

Sandy Koufax once struck out 18 batters in a game. That was an NL record at the time.

Dave McNally's shutout helped the Orioles win their first championship.

Orioles slugger Frank Robinson started Game 1 with a two-run homer. Then teammate Brooks Robinson hit another home run. Just like that, the Orioles led 3–0. But the real star was reliever Moe Drabowsky. Drabowsky came in during the third inning. His best pitch was a fastball, and he used it to strike out 11 batters during the game. Baltimore won 5–2.

Baltimore continued to dominate on the mound. Wally Bunker threw a **complete game** as the Orioles won 1–0 in Game 3. Dave McNally finished off the Series with another **shutout** in Game 4. In total, the Orioles pitchers threw 33 consecutive scoreless innings and outplayed Koufax, Drysdale, and the Dodgers.

FINAL
SERIES
SCORE

ORIOLES | DODGERS

4 | 0

The St. Louis Cardinals won the first two games of the 1985 World Series.

ROYALS TOP CARDINALS

BY 1985, THE ST. LOUIS CARDINALS HAD WON NINE WORLD SERIES. Missouri's other team, the Kansas City Royals, were only in their second World Series and seeking their first win. The Cardinals were heavily favored to win their matchup.

Royals players celebrated together after their historic World Series win.

In Game 6, St. Louis led 1–0 in the bottom of the ninth. A win would **clinch** the series. Then things went wrong. Royals **pinch hitter** Jorge Orta was up to bat. He hit a soft ground ball. Cardinals first baseman Jack Clark picked it up. He flipped it to pitcher Todd Worrell. Worrell made the catch at first before Orta touched the base. However, the umpire called Orta safe. Next Clark missed an important pop foul. Two more batters reached base. Then the Royals' Dane Iorg hit a single to score two runs for the win.

St. Louis still had a chance, but the team struggled in Game 7. The players lacked the concentration they had before. That led to an easy 11–0 win for the Royals. Kansas City had its first World Series title, and it came at the expense of its Missouri rival.

FINAL SERIES SCORE

ROYALS | CARDINALS
4 | 3

METS DEFY EXPECTATIONS

THE 1969 BALTIMORE ORIOLES HAD POWER, PITCHING, AND DEFENSE. The team had easily won the AL. As for the New York Mets? After seven awful seasons, they were finally playing well. But that didn't mean people thought the Mets could really compete with the Orioles in the World Series.

Rookie infielder Wayne Garrett started 98 games for the NL champion New York Mets in 1969.

New York's Donn Clendenon was named the 1969 World Series Most Valuable Player (MVP).

Things began as planned. Baltimore's Mike Cuellar shut the Mets down in a complete game 4–1 win. But then the Mets won Game 2. Before long, the Orioles were trailing three games to one.

The Orioles jumped to a 3–0 lead in Game 5. But the Mets began chipping that lead away. New York's Cleon Jones was on base in the sixth inning. Then Donn Clendenon hit a home run. Al Weis homered in the seventh. Then Ron Swoboda doubled in the eighth inning. His hit brought Jones in to score. Another run from Swoboda, and just like that, the Mets won 5–3. They became the first **expansion team** to win a World Series.

WHAT A CATCH!

Mets outfielder Ron Swoboda made a game-saving catch in Game 4. Trailing by one in the top of the ninth, the Orioles had runners on first and third. There was only one out. Swoboda made a diving grab of a line drive in right field. One run scored on the play, but the runner on first could have scored if the ball had gotten by Swoboda. Instead, the game went to extra innings, and the Mets won.

FINAL SERIES SCORE

METS	ORIOLES
4	1

BASH BROTHERS GET SHUT OUT

THE OAKLAND ATHLETICS CAME INTO THE 1988 WORLD SERIES WITH ALL OF THE FIREPOWER. With sluggers Jose Canseco and Mark McGwire, also known as the "Bash Brothers," the A's had won 104 games. Many expected them to lead Oakland to the championship. The opposing Los Angeles Dodgers, meanwhile, were having a hard time. Their top hitter, Kirk Gibson, could hardly walk due to a hamstring injury.

Game 1 was at Dodger Stadium. Los Angeles' Mickey Hatcher hit a two-run homer in the first inning. But Canseco answered by blasting a grand slam in the second.

Going into the bottom of the ninth inning, the Dodgers still trailed 4–3. Dennis Eckersley was on the mound for Oakland. He needed just one more out. That's when Gibson hobbled to the plate as a pinch hitter. After working a **full count**, he got his pitch. Gibson turned and sent a line drive over the right-field fence. The two-run shot gave Los Angeles the win. Gibson pumped his fist as he slowly made his way around the bases.

Kirk Gibson cheered during his iconic run around the bases.

During the 1988 postseason, Orel Hershiser had a scoreless streak of 22 innings.

After that start, the Dodgers were on a roll. To start Game 2, Orel Hershiser took the mound. The right-handed pitcher was on fire. He had ended the season with five straight shutouts. Hershiser threw a three-hit shutout against the A's. The Dodgers won 6–0.

The Dodgers were thrilled by their improbable win.

Oakland came back to win Game 3 at home. But by then, the Dodgers had momentum. Los Angeles pulled out a 4–3 win in Game 4. Then Hershiser closed things out in Game 5. Although he fell short of another shutout, the Dodgers won 5–2 to claim the World Series title.

FINAL
SERIES
SCORE

DODGERS | A'S
4 | 1

MARLINS SURPRISE YANKEES

THE YANKEES DOMINATED IN THE LATE 1990s. They won the World Series four times in five years. When they met the Florida Marlins in the 2003 World Series, most thought the Yankees would win.

The Marlins, who only began playing in 1993, could hardly match the Yankees' history.

But Florida managed to take Games 1, 4, and 5 to lead the series 3–2. The Marlins needed just one more win.

Florida's Josh Beckett was just 23 years old and pitching in the playoffs for the first time. New York, on the other hand, had Andy Pettitte, a 31-year-old pitching in his thirtieth playoff game.

The home fans were roaring all night. They wanted the Yankees to force Game 7. But Beckett had other ideas. He gave up just five hits and struck out nine in a shutout. The Marlins scored once in the fifth inning and once again in the sixth. Beckett's work on the mound gave the Marlins the outs they needed to lock up the World Series.

Game 6 of the 2003 World Series is sometimes known as the "Josh Beckett Game" for the pitcher's incredible performance.

FINAL SERIES SCORE

MARLINS | YANKEES
4 | 2

The New York Yankees are the Boston Red Sox's biggest rival.

RED SOX TURN THE TABLES

THE BOSTON RED SOX HAD NOT WON A WORLD SERIES SINCE 1918. The New York Yankees had won 26. And when the Yankees won the first three games of the 2004 ALCS, it looked like the same old story.

Dave Roberts was credited for helping the Red Sox rally against the Yankees.

But Game 4 surprised everyone. New York held a 4–3 lead with Mariano Rivera pitching in the ninth inning. A Yankees victory appeared all but certain. Then Boston's Kevin Millar led off with a walk, and **pinch runner** Dave Roberts took his place at first. Roberts went on to steal second base. Bill Mueller followed with a game-tying single.

That sent the game into extra innings. The Red Sox won when David Ortiz hit a two-run homer in the bottom of the 12th inning for a 6–4 victory. The win spurred an epic change in momentum. Boston took the next two games. Game 7 would decide who would represent the AL in the World Series.

Some fans consider David Ortiz's homer in Game 4 to be the greatest moment in his baseball career.

Boston loaded the bases with one out in the top of the second. Star center fielder Johnny Damon greeted Yankees reliever Javier Vazquez by jumping on his first pitch. The long fly ball landed over the fence in right field for a grand slam. The Red Sox were able to hold off New York and completed their upset with a final score of 10–3 in Game 7.

Many people said the Boston Red Sox broke a decades-long curse when they finally won the World Series in 2004.

It was the first time that an MLB team won a playoff series after being down three games to none. The Red Sox advanced to the World Series, where they went on to win for the first time in 86 years.

ON TO THE WORLD SERIES

The Boston Red Sox kept right on going when they played in the World Series against the St. Louis Cardinals. Boston secured a four-game sweep and won eight games in a row overall.

FINAL SERIES SCORE

RED SOX	YANKEES
4	3

ORIOLES MAKE A COMEBACK

THE BALTIMORE ORIOLES WERE GOING THROUGH A BAD SEASON WHEN THEY MET THE BOSTON RED SOX ON JUNE 30, 2009. The Orioles had lost 11 of their last 12 games against Boston. When Boston was up 9–1 by the fifth inning, it appeared Baltimore would lose again.

The Boston Red Sox would go on to have a 95–67 record during 2009.

The Orioles' Robert Andino scored in the bottom of the seventh inning.

The Red Sox scored again in the seventh inning. But the Orioles began to rally, sparked by Oscar Salazar's three-run homer. Baltimore started the bottom of the eighth with four straight hits. A long fly ball and another hit gave the team two more runs.

Baltimore's Nick Markakis came up with two runners on base. He lined the first pitch he saw deep into left-center field. Both runners scored, putting the Orioles on top 11–10.

The Red Sox tried to rally in the ninth. But with two outs, Baltimore pitcher George Sherrill struck out Boston's Jason Bay and closed out an unlikely win.

FINAL SCORE

ORIOLES	RED SOX
11	10

EXTRA INNINGS

THE MLB SEASON IS LONG, WHICH BRINGS MANY OPPORTUNITIES FOR UPSETS AND SURPRISES. There will always be times in baseball when the best teams fall apart. Other times, teams that barely made the playoffs can rally to become champions.

It happens many times in the baseball postseason that the team expected to win doesn't always end up on top.

MLB history is filled with exciting and unpredictable upsets, like when the St. Louis Cardinals defeated the Detroit Tigers in the 2006 World Series.

Originally, only the AL and NL regular-season champions reached the postseason, meeting in the World Series. Then the Championship Series were added, and later the divisional series and the **wild card rounds**. Who knows what changes might come next? However the league is shaped, there are many chances throughout the long baseball season to see incredible matchups and upsets.

GLOSSARY

clinch: when a team gets the number of wins it needs to win a series. A team needs four wins to clinch the World Series title.

complete game: when a pitcher throws an entire game without another pitcher subbing in

expansion team: a new team that is added to a league

favorite: a team expected to win

full count: when the count on a batter is three balls and two strikes

pinch hitter: a player who bats in place of another player

pinch runner: a player who runs in place of a batter who has reached base

rallied: when a team came together and made several hits and scored multiple runs in one inning

shutout: when a single pitcher or team pitches a complete game and does not allow the opposing team to score a run

wild card rounds: postseason games in which two teams that didn't win their divisions face each other for a chance to go up against the number one team in the Division Series

FURTHER INFORMATION

Bechtel, Mark. *Big Book of Who: Baseball.* New York: Liberty Street, 2017.

Bryant, Howard. *Legends: The Best Players, Games, and Teams in Baseball.* New York: Philomel Books, 2015.

Gramling, Gary. *The Baseball Fanbook.* New York: Liberty Street, 2018.

Major League Baseball
www.MLB.com

Science of Baseball
www.exploratorium.edu/baseball

Sports Illustrated Kids: Baseball
https://www.sikids.com/baseball

INDEX

PHOTO ACKNOWLEDGMENTS

The images in this book are used with the permission of: © Chris McGrath/Getty Images Sport/Getty Images, p. 4; © Elsa/Getty Images Sport/Getty Images, p. 6; © John Hefti/Icon Sportswire/Corbis/Getty Images, p. 7; © Bettmann/Getty Images, pp. 8, 9; © AP Images, p. 10; © Focus on Sport/Getty Images, pp. 11, 12, 14, 18, 19; © Rich Pilling/MLB Photos/Getty Images Sport/Getty Images, p. 13; © Herb Scharfman/Sports Imagery/Getty Images Sport/Getty Images, p. 15; © Robert Beck/Icon Sportswire/Getty Images, p. 16; © Joe Kennedy/Los Angeles Times/Getty Images, p. 17; © Linda Cataffo/New York Daily News Archive/Getty Images, p. 20; © Doug Pensinger/Getty Images Sport/Getty Images, pp. 21, 25, 28; © Al Bello/Getty Images Sport/Getty Images, p. 22; © Ezra Shaw/Getty Images Sport/Getty Images, p. 23; © Jim Rogash/WireImage/Getty Images, p. 24; © G Fiume/Getty Images Sport/Getty Images, pp. 26, 27; © Scott Rovak/Getty Images Sport/Getty Images, p. 29.

Front cover: © Brad Mangin/MLB Photos/Major League Baseball/Getty Images, top left; © Jim Rogash/WireImage/Getty Images, top right; © Focus on Sport/Getty Images bottom.